Snake of Gold

by Chitra Soundar and Darshika Varma

W
FRANKLIN WATTS
LONDON • SYDNEY

Jago had a small farm. He tried to sow rice on it. The rice didn't grow.

He tried to grow melons, peas, peanuts.

Nothing grew on his land.

But Jago never gave up.

One day, Jago saw an anthill on the farm.

But there were no ants around.

"This must now belong to

the king of all snakes," thought Jago.

"The cobra."

4

Suddenly, the cobra sprang out.

It spread its hood and hissed loudly.

At first, Jago was frightened.

Then he understood. The cobra was there

to protect his farm.

Jago brought a dish filled with milk
and set it in front of the cobra.

The cobra slithered out
and began to drink the milk.
Jago went back to his house.

The next morning, Jago went to the anthill.

The cobra had drunk all the milk.

Jago saw something shining in the dish.

He picked it up. It was a gold coin.

Thank you for your gift, Cobra,"
said Jago, happily. "Now I can buy food
for my family."
He refilled the dish with milk and
went back to his house.

Every morning Jago fed the cobra.
And every morning, the cobra gave him
a gold coin. A few days passed.
Now Jago had enough money to buy
new clothes and fresh food for his family.

11

Then, one day, Jago had to go on a trip.

He would be gone for two days.

Jago called his eldest son Lolu.

"Lolu, I have an important job for you,"

he said.

"What is it, Father?"asked Lolu.

"It's your job to feed the cobra tomorrow morning," said Jago.

"Yes, father," said Lolu.

"If you find anything on the dish bring it back to the house," said Jago.

"Yes, father," replied Lolu.

Lolu got up early the next morning.

He took a cup of milk to the anthill.

He looked down at the dish.

"A gold coin!" he cried, picking it up.

Then Lolu poured the milk.

The cobra slithered out to drink it.

Then Lolu had a greedy thought.
Maybe there were more gold coins inside
the anthill. He quickly broke down the anthill.
The cobra hissed at Lolu and slithered away.

But there was no gold in the anthill.

"Oh no!" cried Lolu. "What have I done?"

When Jago returned, Lolu told him everything. Jago was angry with his son. "The cobra was helping us," he said.

"I'm sorry, Father," said Lolu. "I was greedy. I wanted us to have more gold."

Jago shook his head.

"We looked after the cobra
and the cobra looked after us," said Jago.
"We should have been happy with what
we had. Soon we will be poor once again."

Story order

Look at these 5 pictures and captions.
Put the pictures in the right order
to retell the story.

1

Lolu tells his father he destroyed the anthill.

2

Jago finds a gold coin in return
for the milk he left for the cobra.

3 Jago buys clothes and food for his family.

4 A cobra appears from the anthill.

5 Jago leaves his son Lolu in charge.

Independent Reading

This series is designed to provide an opportunity for your child to read on their own. These notes are written for you to help your child choose a book and to read it independently.

In school, your child's teacher will often be using reading books which have been banded to support the process of learning to read. Use the book band colour your child is reading in school to help you make a good choice. *Snake of Gold* is a good choice for children reading at Purple Band in their classroom to read independently.

The aim of independent reading is to read this book with ease, so that your child enjoys the story and relates it to their own experiences.

About the book

A poor farmer, Jago, discovers a cobra in his anthill who returns coins of gold for dishes of milk. When Jago has to go away he leaves his son Lolu in charge. But Lolu gets greedy and tries to find more gold by destroying the anthill, leaving his family as poor as they were before.

Before reading

Help your child to learn how to make good choices by asking: "Why did you choose this book? Why do you think you will enjoy it?" Look at the cover together and ask: "What do you think the story will be about?" Ask your child to think of what they already know about the story context. Then ask your child to read the title aloud. Ask: "What do you think the snake has to do with gold? Does the cover picture give you any clues?" Remind your child that they can sound out the letters to make a word if they get stuck.

Decide together whether your child will read the story independently or read it aloud to you.

During reading

Remind your child of what they know and what they can do independently. If reading aloud, support your child if they hesitate or ask for help by telling the word. If reading to themselves, remind your child that they can come and ask for your help if stuck.

After reading

Support comprehension by asking your child to tell you about the story. Use the story order puzzle to encourage your child to retell the story in the right sequence, in their own words. The correct sequence can be found on the next page.

Give your child a chance to respond to the story: "Why does the Cobra help Jago? How do you think Jago felt when he first discovered the cobra? How would you feel?"

Help your child think about the messages in the book that go beyond the story and ask: "What lesson do you think Lolu learns? Do you think Jago also learns any sort of lesson? Why/why not?"

Extending learning

Help your child predict other possible outcomes of the story by asking: "What do you think the cobra would have done if Lolu had not destroyed the anthill?"

In the classroom, your child's teacher may be teaching how to use speech marks when characters are speaking. There are many examples in this book that you could look at with your child. Find these together and point out how the end punctuation (comma, full stop, question mark or exclamation mark) comes inside the speech marks. Ask the child to read some examples out loud, adding appropriate expression.

Franklin Watts
First published in Great Britain in 2021
by The Watts Publishing Group

Copyright © The Watts Publishing Group 2021

Series Editors: Jackie Hamley and Melanie Palmer
Series Advisors and Development Editors: Dr Sue Bodman and Glen Franklin
Series Designers: Peter Scoulding and Cathryn Gilbert

A CIP catalogue record for this book is
available from the British Library.

ISBN 978 1 4451 7397 9 (hbk)
ISBN 978 1 4451 7398 6 (pbk)
ISBN 978 1 4451 8152 3 (ebook)
ISBN 978 1 4451 7399 3 (library ebook)

Printed in China

Franklin Watts
An imprint of
Hachette Children's Group
Part of The Watts Publishing Group
Carmelite House
50 Victoria Embankment
London EC4Y 0DZ

An Hachette UK Company
www.hachette.co.uk

www.franklinwatts.co.uk

FSC
www.fsc.org
MIX
Paper from
responsible sources
FSC® C104740

Answer to Story order: 4,2,3,5,1